The Care & Ke US

A How-to-Say-It Book for Moms

by Dr. Cara Natterson

illustrated by Josée Masse

★ American Girl®

Published by American Girl Publishing
Copyright © 2015 American Girl

Questions or comments? Call 1-800-845-0005,
visit **americangirl.com**, or write to Customer Service,
American Girl, 8400 Fairway Place, Middleton, WI 53562-0497.

Printed in China
15 16 17 18 19 20 21 22 LEO 10 9 8 7 6 5 4 3 2 1

Editorial Development: Darcie Johnston
Art Direction and Design: Gingko Creative and Gretchen Becker
Illustrations: Josée Masse
Production: Jeannette Bailey, Judith Lary, Paula Moon, Kristi Tabrizi
Special thanks to Jane Annunziata, Psy.D.

This book is not intended to replace the advice of or treatment by physicians, psychologists, or other health-care professionals. It should be considered an additional resource only. Questions and concerns about mental or physical health should always be discussed with a doctor or other health-care provider.

Letter to You

Dear Mom,

Your daughter is between two worlds—childhood and adulthood—and everything is changing. Her body is different. So are her friendships. She's got new responsibilities and more schoolwork. She may have sports or other activities after school. And her feelings seem to change every minute.

You probably remember what all this was like—social pressures, friend drama, and feeling uncomfortable in your own changing body. You remember mood swings and worries and wanting more independence. Because you got through it yourself, you're a great resource for your daughter. And because you love her and want the best for her, you *want* to be that resource for her.

The Care & Keeping of Us can help. This book gives you tools to talk with your daughter about the things most on her mind and yours: body basics and puberty problems, food and fashion, friends and family. You'll find essential information plus wording suggestions for when you're not sure how to open a conversation or respond to a request. Look for the "How to Say It?" bubbles on every page, and adapt them to fit your own situation.

You don't have to already know every answer. You won't need to come up with an instant solution for every problem. But you can listen. You can share and be supportive. You can help her make decisions that are safe or smart, or that feel right. And when you need to say no or set a limit, you can do so in ways that tell her you respect her growing independence. More than simply answering a question or solving a problem, your goal is making a habit of comfortable communication.

Here's how.

Your friends at American Girl

Contents

Conversation Starters

How do you begin? When there's something on your mind—or you can see there's something on your daughter's mind—how do you start a conversation with her? All kinds of things can make it hard . . .

✳ Maybe you feel awkward or embarrassed when talking about the body or private matters.

✳ Maybe you know your daughter feels uncomfortable talking about it, too.

✳ Maybe you're worried your daughter will react negatively, and you'd rather avoid it.

✳ Maybe you've tried to talk about something before without success, and you feel discouraged.

✳ Maybe you don't know why you think or feel the way you do, and you want to know your own mind before you start talking.

✳ Maybe you feel ineffective or foolish, regardless of how clear you are.

✳ Maybe you're afraid of losing your cool.

✳ Maybe for conversations this personal you want time and privacy that are hard to come by.

✳ Maybe your daughter is in a good mood, and you don't want to ruin it.

Here are some icebreakers that can get a conversation going:

"It's been a while since we talked about _____. I've had a chance to think about it and maybe you have, too. Let's go for a walk and share our thoughts."

"This probably feels really embarrassing to talk about. I remember feeling embarrassed with my mom when talking about it. But I can see you're worried, and I'd like to help."

"I can tell something's bothering you. Would you like to use me as a sounding board? I'd be happy to listen, and maybe if you talk it through you'll come up with some ideas or even just feel better."

"Let's go out for lunch this weekend, just you and me. We've been wanting to try that new pizza place, and I'd love to spend some fun time with just you."

...& Stoppers

Sometimes a conversation takes a wrong turn, especially when emotions run high. Feeling upset can trigger unproductive reactions such as yelling, sarcasm, withdrawing emotionally, unreasonable punishment, overcontrolling, and just walking away. If that happens, you end up getting nowhere, and both of you feel bad—angry, humiliated, unappreciated, unloved, misunderstood, or regretful.

How do you handle it when you feel your emotions heating up? What do you say? What do your face and body language say? Certain responses are more likely to shut down communication than keep it going:

Your daughter is a unique individual with ideas and opinions of her own. She will say things you don't appreciate or agree with, and that's OK. You want her to feel able to voice her thoughts, because that's essential to her becoming an independent person with a well-developed sense of self. Your challenge is to keep your cool and stay on track until you have a plan or she feels better or the problem is solved—whatever your goal may be.

Talking Tips

There is no "right" way or best time to talk to your daughter about puberty, but here are some tips to make your conversations go more smoothly.

※ Mood matters. Try to pick a time when neither of you is tired, busy, or stressed.

※ Create a comfy, private space. Offer a favorite drink or snack, or play music in the background that you both enjoy. Choose a good time and a place where you won't be overheard.

※ Plan special times together. A one-on-one in a nice setting is a natural chance for private conversation, and having fun together makes the bond between you stronger.

※ One thing at a time. Don't feel like you have to cover everything in one conversation, and be sensitive if your daughter's attention or interest starts to drift.

※ *Breeeeathe.* If you feel yourself getting upset, take a slow, deep breath. And another.

※ Visualize your best self. Picture the mom you want to be—your word choices, your tone of voice, the look on your face. Or picture someone else you know who seems to keep her cool in a way that feels right to you. Then try to be her.

※ Take a break. If you're not ready to make a decision, say so: "Let's talk again tomorrow morning, after I've had a chance to think about it some more." Then be sure to follow up.

※ Research. "I don't know" is a fine answer. If you don't know what to say, get back to her—or if you need information, make it fun to look it up together.

※ Reset. If you lose your cool, don't be afraid to say, "I'm sorry I said that. Where were we?"

※ Laugh together! Laughing that is truly shared is a terrific stress buster and bonding agent.

※ Fizzle before fixing. If possible, let a charged situation settle down before talking about it.

※ Listen sensitively. Avoid interrupting, but do respond after she's poured her heart out.

※ Honor honesty. Honesty is essential in any relationship. Being open and truthful creates trust and fosters respect, integrity, and maturity.

※ Remember your job description. Your job is to see to your daughter's health, safety, learning, and emotional well-being, and to help her toward a happy and productive adulthood. It's OK to say no and to be unpopular from time to time.

✳ It's in there. Tell yourself that even if she didn't seem to hear it, she did.

✳ Start early. The sooner she gets used to talking about her body, her feelings, and her life, the more practice you'll have for when it's harder and more complicated.

✳ Put yourself in your daughter's shoes. Try to understand what motivates her and what unnerves her. If you aren't sure, ask; this will help show that you care. You can be sympathetic and understanding without permitting or agreeing to something.

✳ Consider her collaboration style. Your daughter may respond better if she's given a chance to first work on a plan herself, before reviewing it with you. Some kids hear parental feedback better if they are the originators of an initial plan.

✳ Take a hike. Walking together often helps people open up.

✳ It doesn't have to be face-to-face. Some conversations are more comfortable when you can avoid eye contact, such as in the car, at bedtime in the dark, or when walking the dog.

✳ Offer a network. All kids do best if they have several trusted adults in their lives. Give your daughter a list of people—other parents, family members, adult friends, school counselors, or members of your faith—who can give her advice or explain things in ways that align with your value system.

✳ Model. The things you tell your children for health and safety are just as important for you—and your daughter is much more likely to follow your actions than your words.

Your Past

How much about your past is appropriate to share with your tween daughter? If she's wondering about her changing body or how to handle something, telling her about your experience can be a great way to offer ideas. But certain details may not be helpful at her age. If she asks questions that feel too personal, you have a perfect opportunity to teach good boundaries by not sharing too much information—a vital skill in this era of social media. You might say, "Those details wouldn't be helpful for you, but tell me more about what's on your mind. Maybe I can help in a better way." At the same time, anything you choose to tell her should be disclosed only because she asks and wants to know, not because you feel like sharing it. If she seems uncomfortable or uninterested in a story about your past, or she asks you to stop, gently change the subject.

Body Talk

Your daughter's body is changing. Some girls (and their moms) think it's happening too fast. Some girls feel like it isn't happening soon enough. No matter the timeline, though, it is happening.

No doubt, you remember what it felt like to go through puberty. It was kind of fun, but also awkward and vulnerable. As you changed, you watched your friends experience growth spurts and pimples and needing bras, sometimes on the same schedule as you but not always. Your daughter is living and witnessing these transitions now. Along with all of these body changes come lots of questions: How tall will she be? When will she get her period? How should she deal with body hair or body odor? Is she normal? Parents and kids often think and wonder about the same things, but aren't always sure how to talk about them.

These days, many parents also wonder about the bigger picture: Why does everything seem to be happening sooner than it used to? And why does it seem more complicated? The world has indeed changed a lot since you were a child. Puberty begins a year or two sooner for both boys and girls. Not only that, everything surrounding puberty is also happening earlier: the expectation that a child will act and look more "grown up," that she'll be interested in things like popular music and romantic crushes, and that she will give up toys and other childhood things. This early entry into puberty means that both girls and their moms have less time to prepare for it emotionally. This can feel like a loss because your daughter has less time to just be a little girl.

Something that often helps mothers and daughters navigate this challenging transition is to focus on healthy living. Healthy living is about health, not weight or height or clothing size or style. It's not about speeding up social or emotional maturity. The emphasis redirects the focus away from common concerns like "Am I thin enough?" and "Are my clothes cool?" It means making daily choices that respect the body: putting healthy foods in and keeping the junk out, working out hard, and also allowing yourself to rest.

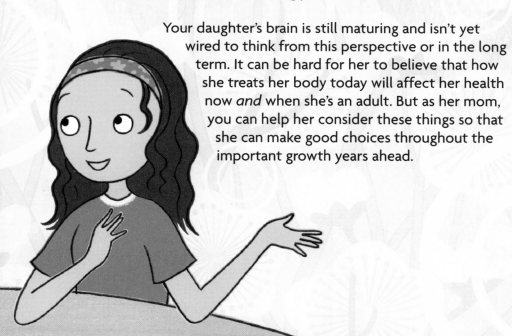

Your daughter's brain is still maturing and isn't yet wired to think from this perspective or in the long term. It can be hard for her to believe that how she treats her body today will affect her health now *and* when she's an adult. But as her mom, you can help her consider these things so that she can make good choices throughout the important growth years ahead.

Hygiene Basics

Hygiene is another word for keeping clean and healthy. Self-care and self-esteem are interconnected. When a girl likes the way she looks, she is likely to feel happier and more confident, and that helps her put her best foot forward in the world. This is especially important during puberty, when body changes make girls feel less sure of themselves. Now that your daughter is getting older, she'll want to pay more attention to hygiene.

How to Say It?
"I know you hate it when I keep reminding you to take a shower. I don't like it either. I feel like I'm nagging you, and nobody likes that. Is there some other way you can think of that I could help you get into a routine?"

How to Say It?
"I'm really proud of how you're taking charge of your routine in the morning, and it's great that you want to look your best. It seems like you don't have the time you need to get ready, though. Would you like to wake up a little earlier? You might feel less stressed and rushed. Or is there something else you can think of that would help?"

She also *needs* to care more. One of the earliest changes in puberty is an increase in the production of oil and sweat, which can cause odors, rashes, an oily scalp, and acne. Of course, the best defense against extra sweat and oil is to wash well with gentle soaps, shampoos, and cleansers. Each girl has her own timeline, not only with physical changes but also with her interest in personal hygiene and grooming. Some girls are eager to develop a self-care routine; others may need more guidance and support.

Either way, she can use your help in learning how to take care of herself and establish a routine—even if she seems not to want it. But how do you avoid feeling that you're always reminding her? Eventually she will take responsibility for her hygiene, but until she does, here are a few ways you can help her get there.

Go shopping together. Help her choose a facial cleanser and moisturizer made for her skin type, shampoo for her hair type, and a gentle soap or shower gel. Before you shop, talk about products

How to Say It?
"I was thinking about going shopping for some new soap and shampoo for you, now that you're older. We could check out what's recommended for your skin and hair type, and then you could pick some things you might like to try."

she'll need. She may want to do her own research so that she feels more ownership. This can help you avoid conflict, and if it's fun, she's more likely to enjoy these new responsibilities.

Show her how it's done. Set aside time to show or talk through how to wash her face, take care of her hair, and bathe her changing body. Demonstrate washing your own face, for example, or watch an online video. Read the directions on her products. Go through some general tips, such as rinsing well—whether it's soap, shampoo, or conditioner. Her doctor may have some information sheets or online recommendations, too. Don't try to do it all at once, and keep it light and fun. Your daughter might feel talked down to and object that she knows how to do all this, so start by explaining that the products or care practices she needs now are different from what she's been used to.

Ask someone else. If your daughter is reluctant or resists your suggestions, you might get an assist from her favorite aunt, an older sister or cousin, or someone else she knows well, respects, and likes.

Help her set up a routine. Together create a list of hygiene tasks for her to follow, or help her refine a list that she has created independently. Find a place where she can post it, ideally in the bathroom. Make a place for her products where they are easy to see and to use.

Ask her if she has any ideas about how you can help her remember. She knows what might help her the most. Even if it's more reminders from you, they won't feel like nagging if they come at her own request.

How to Say It?
"These products will work a little differently from the ones you've been using. I know you've been washing your face and shampooing your hair for years, but now that you're older, I thought I would pass on a few tips for how to keep your complexion and hair looking their best."

Already on Board?
Your daughter may already have good hygiene habits. In your family, the issue may be that she wants to spend time on personal care but she needs help managing that time. Does she need to get up earlier to get ready for school? Does there need to be a bathroom schedule for the family? Take a practical look at the problems and talk them through together. If she knows you respect her desire to take care of her body and feel good about how she looks, she'll be more likely to help with compromises and solutions.

Nutrition

Part of the recipe for feeling, doing, and even looking one's best is eating right. A body needs a balance of proteins, grains, fruits, vegetables, fats, vitamins, and minerals to grow and be strong. That's true for both kids and adults.

Most kids can't think in terms of eating food that's good for their growing bodies. Instead, they want foods that taste good. They often want familiar foods, not even a new version of an old favorite. Maybe they eat a limited menu—only pizza, jelly sandwiches, and bananas. Or they can't mix foods on the plate. Or absolutely no veggies!

How to Say It?

"I know it's annoying if I say you can't have dessert until you finish your dinner. I felt the same way when I was your age and my parents would say the same thing. But filling up on dessert means there's less room—and less desire—for healthy food that's good for your body."

How to Say It?

"Let's talk about what you'd like to take to school in your lunch. What kinds of things are your favorites—but are nutritious, too? Would you like to come to the grocery store with me and pick out some things?"

Your job is to ease your daughter into understanding that food is about making choices for her health as well as pleasure. She has been listening to you tell her to eat this or drink that for as long as she can remember. Now she's old enough to take charge of some of her own habits, and that will feel good for both of you. It's true that she doesn't buy the food in your house—her parents do. But she can get involved in the choices you make.

Start by talking about her likes and dislikes. What are some of her favorite foods? What are foods that she doesn't like all that much but knows she should eat anyway? Does she eat breakfast? (She should, and you might need to explain why.) Does she buy school lunch or take her

Super Sips

Drinks matter! Both kids and adults consume too many empty calories in sodas, juices, and energy drinks, some of which deliver the equivalent of two or three candy bars' worth of sugar. Even water can be confusing. If the liquid in the bottle is colorful or sweet, it contains some combination of sugars, artificial ingredients, and calories. "Juice" can be misleading. too. Choose "100% juice" over a "juice drink," or better yet, opt for milk or pure water. For something a little fancier, try adding 100% OJ, fresh lemon, or mint leaves to plain seltzer.

own? If she buys, what does she choose? If she takes a lunch, what's in the bag or box? What kinds of snacks does she like to eat?

Then talk about healthy foods, and make some decisions together. Start with the healthy things she already likes, and build on those. Suggest you do some research together, online or at the library, to find out some of the science behind good nutrition—and why it matters to her now. Make grocery lists and go to the market together. Go to a bookstore and pick out a couple of cookbooks that appeal to both of you; a cookbook for kids or teens that she can follow is best. Invite her to help plan and prepare family dinners. Her tastes will develop, she'll learn about nutrition, she'll gain cooking skills, and the two of you will have opportunities to talk and laugh together.

Healthy Diets

The word *diet* simply means "what you eat." Some diets are healthy, some are not. A healthy diet includes all the good foods a body needs in the right amounts, and it limits sugary, fried, and processed foods. When shopping together, teach your daughter to read food labels. One easy way to spot processed foods is if the ingredients include chemicals that regular people don't keep in their kitchen. Another simple rule is to count the number of ingredients. Generally, the lower the number, the healthier the food.

HUMMUS

Exercise

Exercise. Working out. Physical activity. Moving your body. No matter what you call it, it makes the body and the brain feel great and reduces stress, too. Exercise helps blood flow to muscles and organs, refreshing the whole body while keeping it fit. It also can have profound effects on mood: If you're anxious about something and you take an exercise break, the worry often turns into a focus on problem solving. It always feels better to get up and move. Exercise even helps you sleep better and perform better at work and school. If your daughter is complaining about how much you prompt her to get up and move, that's not so bad. It means you already know there are so many good reasons for being active. The challenge, of course, is helping your daughter learn this, too, and feel the benefits of exercise firsthand.

How to Say It?
"I'm glad you're thinking about ways to get exercise, and I think your idea to try tennis is great. You've tried other things and had trouble sticking with it. How about you research some lesson options and tell me what looks best to you. Then you could make a commitment to four or eight weeks of classes. What do you think?"

Exercise comes in many forms: working out in a class, playing sports, dancing, bike riding, bowling, swimming, hiking, gardening, walking the dog—just about anything other than sitting around counts. Interests change over time, and kids in particular like to explore new activities. If you have a hunch about a sport or workout your girl might enjoy, share this with her. You may have ideas she never considered before. You may also stumble on something new that you'll enjoy, too. Whether it's a competitive sport or something solo and just for fun, she's a winner if she's doing it, and so are you.

Motion Monitor

If you and your daughter want a fun way to see how much exercise you're getting, try a wireless device or an app that keeps track of physical activity. Even a simple step counter can be a great motivator to move!

Being an active exerciser yourself gives your daughter a great role model for the joys and benefits—and it will help you cope with the stress of having a daughter entering puberty.

Everyone needs to exercise daily—both kids and adults. It's a key part of healthy living. An hour a day is recommended for everyone, and it can be done all at once or scattered throughout the day. Any amount of exercise will reduce stress and refresh

Too Much?

If your daughter is actually getting more than 60 minutes of exercise a day, that's great, but don't let her push it too far. Excessive exercise can lead to injury or unhealthy weight loss. If you're concerned that your daughter is having trouble finding the right balance, share this with her and help her gauge when she is pushing herself too hard. Also, don't hesitate to turn to her gym teacher, pediatrician, school nurse, or coach if you think she's overdoing it and needs the perspective of someone outside the family. If you are having trouble finding balance in your own routine, seek out support for yourself, too. You're an important role model for your girl. If she sees you treating your body in an unhealthful way, she may think she should do the same. Of course, the opposite is also true. The more she sees you taking good care of yourself, the easier it will be for her to do the same.

the brain and body. In school, kids spend many hours at their desks, and once they are home they do homework, watch TV, and spend time online. All this means a lot of sitting, which in turn means an even greater need for a commitment to exercise. But just as adults find reasons not to work out, tweens find ways to resist, too . . .

It's boring! It feels like a chore! If you hear this in your house, talk about ways to make it fun (and do this regularly). Also talk about how good people feel once they find exercise they like and get themselves up and moving. You can also come up with an incentive chart that includes goals and prizes.

I don't have time. Between school, homework, and activities, your daughter might indeed need help fitting in exercise. Look at her schedule with her, and set priorities together.

It hurts. Some girls complain of pain when they exercise. If your daughter says something hurts, call her doctor. There might be a physical injury or problem that needs attention. On the other hand, she might be worried about unfamiliar aches and pains of her changing body, and just needs to talk them through.

How to Say It?
"I know we talk a lot about how important exercise is for feeling good and helping with stress. I was thinking if you tried something that you really enjoyed, exercising might seem more fun. When you went to camp last year, you really liked the horseback riding and dance classes. What do you think about looking into these activities? Or do you have other ideas?"

How to Say It?
"How about doing a mother/daughter yoga class with me? It could be good exercise, and I think it would be fun to try something new together."

Sleep

The notion of healthy living includes sleep as much as daytime choices like getting enough exercise and eating well. Sleep is key for your daughter's growth and metabolism. It's restorative, allowing stress hormones to subside and emotions to reset. And during sleep, what she learned during the day is organized and stored in memory. Without enough sleep, kids can suffer from lower grades in school and increased moodiness. (This all applies to moms, too, who need sleep to build their own resilience so that they can parent effectively during this challenging stage in their daughters' lives.)

How to Say It?
"I've been hearing some interesting research about sleep and what happens when we don't get enough. You've probably learned about sleep in health class, too. I'm curious to know if what we're learning helps you decide to turn off the lights earlier or get more rest."

But getting enough sleep is often easier said than done. Her life is filled with school and homework, activities, family time, socializing, meals, chores, and more. She might be staying up too late getting it all done, or she could be sleeping poorly because she's worrying about her load. Most families need to set limits and establish priorities to keep balance in their lives, and parents need to take the lead. Talking about what's most important and deciding what can be deferred or let go is a good family practice.

How to Say It?
"Most parents have a rule that all screens and devices have to be turned off one hour before you go to bed. The problem with screens is that the light wakes up your brain, making it harder to fall asleep. Getting enough sleep is so important for feeling good and doing well."

Another culprit is screen time. The light emitted from many screens—particularly computers and mobile devices—is known to stimulate the brain, waking it up and making it more difficult to fall asleep. Increasingly, though, tweens do their homework, socialize, and play using screens, sometimes up to the moment when they go to bed. The solution is to set a rule that all screens are turned off at least an hour before bed—and to explain why. When kids understand the reason for a rule, they are much more likely to follow it.

If she has trouble falling asleep, here are some helpful tips:

Go to bed at the same time every night. The brain and body will learn to anticipate that it's time for sleep and will start to wind down.

Follow the same routine at night. This also trains the brain for sleep. In addition to washing up, brushing teeth, and changing into pj's, her routine might include a bath, journaling, reading, or listening to soothing music or an audiobook.

Try focusing on your breath or learning to meditate. Many tools are available to teach relaxation and deep breathing. These are especially helpful for kids who have trouble falling asleep as a result of anxiety.

Conversations about sleep can quickly turn contentious. Beginning in the toddler years, many kids fight sleep because they think they will miss something. When you talk to your daughter about sleep routines, first acknowledge her concern that she'll miss out on something important, and then focus on the benefits of rest: better grades in school, feeling happier, feeling less stressed, being able to respond better to problems, and even looking better. Help her want to turn off the lights.

How to Say It?

"You've been looking kind of tired lately, and I wonder if you're getting enough sleep. I know that kids your age have a lot to keep up with and don't want to miss out on anything. But that's why it's so important to fuel yourself with sleep. Let's think about how to address this. For example, maybe you could try getting to bed 20 minutes earlier and see if you feel more refreshed."

How to Say It?

"It's terrific that you're so conscientious about your homework, but staying up an extra hour isn't a good option. You're already so tired, I don't think you can do quality work now, and we have agreed on a lights-out time. How about trying some deep breathing to help you fall asleep, and setting your alarm a half hour earlier? You'll be better rested when you tackle your homework."

Insomnia?

It's common to develop anxiety around sleep troubles: Not being able to fall asleep can cause worry, which in turn makes sleep even harder to come by. Parents don't always know if a child isn't sleeping well. If you suspect your daughter isn't getting enough sleep, ask her. Then figure out together what might be keeping her up and work out a plan for a better night's sleep. Your pediatrician can help with your plan, too.

Safety

Safety rules can seem silly or downright annoying to the tween or teen brain. *Put on your helmet! Buckle up! Put on sunscreen!* You may find yourself repeating these warnings over and over in your home.

Ultimately, being safe means having respect for yourself and your body. As you communicate this to your daughter, help her to understand the wide range of circumstances when she needs to consider her safety. Protecting herself from injury is just one form of safe thinking. As she gets older, there will be others, including avoiding harmful substances, staying away from unsafe places, and behaving cautiously online.

How to Say It?
"I understand that you're getting older and that you're smart and responsible. I'm really proud of how mature you're becoming. But it's not safe for you to be at the mall alone with friends until you're older. In a year or two, we can see how things are going and revisit the issue."

When it comes to safety rules, there shouldn't be much room for negotiation. Black-and-white rules help kids make better decisions when parents aren't around. Clear rules can also help kids offer up an excuse: "My mom said I can't do that, and I will get in a lot of trouble if I do" is one way for a child to get out of an uncomfortable or potentially dangerous situation. It also matters that you follow the rules as well: Your daughter is most likely to do as you do, not as you say.

Many kids push back. Often they simply don't understand why the rules exist. Sometimes the resistance is just part of getting older and wanting a little more independence. Sometimes they think parents worry too much. Most of all, though, they tend to believe something bad can't happen to them.

There's a biological reason behind this belief. The part of the brain that makes decisions, weighs consequences and risks, and considers

Changing Rules

Some rules, such as seat belt use, are for life. Others may change. As your daughter gets older and more responsible, you'll make adjustments. But it's also OK to go back to an earlier or stricter rule if you think you've made a mistake. Acknowledge that you tried something but realized it wasn't working, it wasn't safe enough, or you didn't have all the information. This process is often easier for everyone if you present a new rule like this: "We are trying something new" (or changing an old rule, or testing out a new way of doing something). If it works well and we're both comfortable, we'll keep the change in place, at least for now. If it doesn't work well, we'll go back to the old rule and try again in a few months."

the long term won't be fully developed until age 25 or later. Your daughter doesn't have to be a risk taker or reckless—even if she's cautious, she still doesn't have the ability to think as clearly as you do. Clear rules that don't give her room to wiggle or argue will help keep her safe as she's becoming more independent.

It's important that your daughter understands the reasons behind the limits. Her still-developing tween brain isn't wired to think through long-term consequences, but if you explain them to her, she can better appreciate the rules. When rules make sense and don't seem arbitrary, everyone—kids and adults—is far more likely to uphold them.

How to Say It?
"You've been asking for time at home alone. Let's start with 20 minutes, with me being very close by, and see how it goes. If it works well, great. If we're not both comfortable, we'll stick with the rule of a grown-up always at home and just try again in a few months."

How to Say It?
"Now that you're getting older, you'll be making more decisions on your own. Let's talk about how you can handle it when a friend wants to do something that might be risky, and you know it breaks one of our safety rules. Let's say you're at a friend's house and she wants to bake cookies. But her parent isn't home, and we have a rule that an adult has to be there if you use the oven or stove. How can you keep yourself safe in that situation? What could you say to your friend?"

Puberty Firsts

Your daughter's body will transform during puberty, but exactly what will happen first or when it will start is impossible to know in advance. Some girls get pubic hair first and breasts later, while others do the opposite. Some girls start the process as early as age 7, while others are already teens. And it's all normal.

A girl may follow about the same timeline or sequence as her mother, but not always. Your daughter may be more like another family member. Environment plays a role, too. And if she's adopted, her biological history simply may not be available.

How to Say It?
"How are things going? You and your friends have a lot going on now. I know we've talked about puberty and the different emotional and physical changes that go with it, and you've done some reading, too. Do you have any questions? Would it be helpful if I told you a little bit about what it was like for me when I was your age?"

The lack of predictability is a source of anxiety for many girls, and they often compare their development. If your daughter is developing later than her friends, she may feel impatient. If she starts earlier, she may feel rushed and sad and want to hide it. When girls are either early or late—or even when they're absolutely average in their timing— they worry, feel embarrassed, and wonder if they are normal. One comfortable way to ask your daughter how she feels about her progress through puberty is to offer to share your own story.

How to Say It?
"Now that you're getting older and your body is starting to change, you'll need new basic clothes, including underwear. I'm thinking it's about time to start looking at bras. You'll feel more comfortable with a bra, and your clothes will look and fit better, too. What if we make bra shopping part of our next shopping trip?"

Girls anticipate—and sometimes dread—the appearance of breasts. They're both excited and embarrassed because this change is noticeable by others. Some moms wait for their daughters to bring up the subject or ask for a bra, because they're concerned that their girls will feel humiliated. Odds are, though, your daughter wants to talk about it but feels too awkward to bring it up, or she doesn't realize that talking about it will help resolve her worries. You can help her get comfortable with her changing body by gently approaching her.

Bra Time?

Your daughter's first bra might be a training bra, a sports bra, or a cup bra. When you both agree it's time, get off to the right start by visiting a shop where knowledgeable staff can help you choose the right type and fit for her. This experience is one she'll probably remember for a long time, so do your best to help it go smoothly. Choose a store where staff are used to working with first-time bra shoppers, and follow the trip with something fun such as a movie or snack.

Those body changes include hair, too. Body hair will appear in new places for your daughter—under the arms and in the pubic area—and it will grow thicker on the arms and legs. Some girls don't care. Others feel more self-conscious or even unattractive. Moms may avoid talking about hair altogether because they're concerned that the talk will go straight to hair removal. But many girls are just curious or they simply want acknowledgment. They aren't necessarily looking to remove the hair. If your daughter is in fact starting to wonder about hair removal, you'll want to answer her questions about methods and talk about when she'll be old enough.

Decisions about hair removal are based on personal feelings inspired by cultural norms. Hair is healthy, and women view it and treat it differently in different parts of the world. In your discussions with your daughter, talking about other views can help her understand that hair removal is more a cultural choice than a true hygiene issue. This may take some of the pressure off for both of you—besides giving you a fascinating topic to explore together.

How to Say It?

"I'm glad you told me how you feel. I understand what it's like to feel like others are looking at the hair on your legs. Yes, we can talk about options for hair removal at your age. I don't want you to feel uncomfortable about it."

Periods

In general, girls are entering puberty sooner than their moms did. But they aren't getting their periods at younger ages. In fact, the average age for a first period is still 12½, about the same as a generation ago. Talking about when you first got your period is a great way to open the conversation with your daughter. Will she start at the same age as you? That's as good a guess as any—but one that isn't always accurate. Some girls will get their periods a year or two sooner (or later) than their moms did.

Most girls have some anxiety about getting their first period. Anything new that's this significant can be scary because it's an unknown. Also, the thought of blood can be worrisome because until now your daughter has associated blood with an injury or with something bad. Add to that the fear of pain, and possibly the vision that her period will come while she's wearing white shorts at school. Any and all of these things could be on her mind.

You can help. Talk with her about your own experience, including describing how you felt before getting your period. She'll probably respond with her own feelings, giving you the chance to be supportive and reassuring. You can also relieve many of her worries by giving her basic information and taking some practical steps.

Describe her first period. Let her know that the first periods will probably be light. Even once she's had it for a while, the total amount of blood lost will only be about three tablespoons. Have her measure that much water into a cup so that she can see her flow will be manageable.

How to Say It?
"Even though it could be a while before you start your period, I was thinking this might be a good time to get you some supplies. That way you can feel prepared. How about going shopping together for supplies to keep at home and in your backpack? It might also be a good time to sit down together and talk about anything that's on your mind about starting your period."

How to Say It?
"I remember how nervous I felt before getting my period. When I was about your age, not knowing what to expect was the hardest part. I was also bothered by not knowing when and where it would start and what it would feel like. But it turned out to be much easier than I imagined."

Get products. Purchase pads and pantyliners now, so that she will have them on hand. Have her decide where she'd like to keep them. Take a look at the products together, and show her how she'll use and dispose of them, and how often she'll change them.

Assemble a Period Kit. Put together a kit of necessities for your daughter to keep in the bottom of her backpack starting now, so she'll be ready at any time. Use a small zipper pouch, such as a cosmetic or pencil case, and include a pad, a change of panties, a plastic baggie, and a travel packet of wipes. If she's open to it, do this together.

Be available. You can be a tremendous source of information for your daughter after her period begins, too. Cramps, using pads versus tampons, figuring out when the next period is coming—the questions won't end when her first period begins. When she asks for more supplies, that's a great time to ask how it's going. She'll be glad to know you're there as a reliable and sympathetic resource.

How to Say It?
"It's hard to be one of the first to get your period. The good news is that everyone gets it eventually, and then you won't think about how uncomfortable you're feeling. You don't have to tell anyone, but you should probably get used to the idea that your friends are likely to find out. The best way to handle it is to just be very matter-of-fact. You could say something like, 'Yep, I started my period. I guess it'll be happening to all of us soon.'"

How to Say It?
"Cramps are a really common worry. I do remember cramps being uncomfortable sometimes. But there are some really easy tricks to making them feel better. Eating healthy food and exercising can reduce cramp pain. And if it still feels like too much, there are medicines that help a lot."

Her Changing Shape

Your daughter's body will change shape during puberty, perhaps dramatically. Some girls become quite curvaceous while others have longer, straighter figures; some will have their mom's build while others will be shaped entirely differently.

Of all the changes in puberty, changing shape is possibly the most complicated. A girl's new curves—whether small or large—will make her look older, and she may or may not be happy about that. Curves are also complicated because they are connected to issues of body image, size and weight, and standards of beauty.

How to Say It?
"This is a pretty complicated time. So much is changing—your feelings, some of your interests, and your figure, too. You're starting to look like a young woman. I remember being excited about it but then feeling really self-conscious and unsure of myself. I think we all do—guys too! Change can be hard, but it's also exciting, and I'm really proud of what a great young woman you're becoming."

As your daughter's shape changes, she will start to see herself differently. Some days, she might feel absolutely great—it's exciting to get taller and look more grown up. But other days she might feel insecure, not ready to grow up, imagining everyone in the world is staring and judging her. These feelings can be triggered when she's putting on clothes at home and they don't fit right anymore, or when she's out shopping and styles and sizes she used to wear don't look the same. She may be unhappy that she needs a larger size to accommodate her new curves, or she might be excited to see and admire her new shape.

How to Say It?
"I felt like you do when I was your age—not just about the changes in my body but also the way my feelings seemed to flip-flop. I would like feeling and looking more mature one day; then the next day I'd wish I could go back to being a kid. What helped was remembering that there was no rush to grow up, and that I could still enjoy things I liked when I was younger. It also helped when I remembered that my friends were probably dealing with the very same feelings."

Eyes on Her?
"Wow, she looks so grown up!" You don't want your daughter to feel like she should *hide* these changes, but she might feel embarrassed when other people make comments, even if those comments are well-intended. Help her plan some responses, such as a simple "thank you" or redirecting the conversation away from her looks. You might also suggest clothing that makes her feel good without attracting attention she doesn't want.

Different Bodies?

It's natural for girls to compare their figures, height, and overall look to their moms'. Some are shaped like their mothers and may cultivate a similar style, giving them common ground—although it can lead to more comparing, too. Other girls have different genes from their moms, and if they aren't happy with how they look, they may wish they looked more like their mom, who seems so put together. They can also worry that their mom can't understand what it's like to be them. Giving your daughter perspective is most helpful. Remind her that you've had many years to find your style. As she gets older, she'll have time to evolve her own style as well.

It's natural for a mother to have mixed feelings, too: pride in her daughter's growing maturity, wistfulness about her little girl growing up or the loss of her own youth, and even worries about sexual attention. Talking with other moms can be a great help. If feelings persist or get in the way of good parenting, though, mention them to someone you trust and can talk to for guidance..

It's normal for her confidence to flip-flop. You probably remember what it was like to feel on top of the world one minute and awkward the next. When she's feeling self-conscious about her body, letting her know you understand can be quite comforting. She may ask you how you felt about looking older and how people around you reacted. Hearing your stories that are humorous, inspiring, or reassuring can make all the difference in how she feels. Talking about her own feelings will also help her work through them and get perspective. Her feelings of self-doubt and self-consciousness won't disappear forever, but you can help her think things through so that she feels more comfortable and confident most of the time.

How to Say It?

"You might have mixed feelings when people say how much you're growing up. Part of you probably likes hearing how you look and act more mature, but another part may not like so much focus on your looks. Sometimes the simplest response is the best: Just smile and say thanks and move on. You could also change the focus away from you with something like, 'Thank you, and how are you?' or 'Thanks, and what's new with you?'"

Beauty & Style

Images of women can influence our ideas about what we should look like. They often look perfect—and oftentimes unhealthy. These images, in the media and advertising, create standards of beauty that are unattainable. Real people don't look like that. But it's easy to forget and to believe what you see.

Your daughter's self-esteem and her physical health will benefit from on-going conversations about how we define beauty in our society. Make it a point to talk about girls and women she knows, and what makes them beautiful. Is it their bodies and makeup? Or is it their minds, their laughter, or the warmth in their eyes?

How to Say It?
"The better you feel about the way you look, the less you'll notice and be bothered by how other girls and women look. Let's talk about what you wish was different and maybe make some decisions that can address your concerns. But keep in mind that almost everyone dislikes a thing or two about the way she looks. Let's also focus on all the good things about you, and how attractive you really are, even though you may not always believe it."

Explore ideas of beauty in different parts of the world, too. Try to find cultures that appreciate healthy bodies, and discuss how broad and flexible the definition of "beauty" really is. Discuss how media images affect the way both of you feel about yourselves. What's the difference between an "ideal" body and a healthy one? Talk about how she might create her own definition of beauty. What's a realistic, happy, healthy look for her?

How to Say It?
"Let's start with an eye doctor appointment and see if you're a good candidate for contacts. We can also find out the pros and cons of contacts and glasses, and how much they cost. And let's look at new glasses that you think are more flattering. Then we can talk about the next steps."

As your daughter grows and changes, so will the look she cultivates for herself. Her look will eventually include choices for such things as hair and makeup. It will include clothing and accessories such as jewelry, footwear, and eyeglasses versus contacts. She'll probably experiment with various styles—sporty, classic, natural, preppy, a color theme, a time period, and so forth. Whatever her look, you'll want her to feel good about herself as you help her shape a sense of beauty that's healthy and real.

Face

It's not uncommon for girls to focus on the parts of themselves they don't like, particularly features of their face. Makeup, they often think, can make everything look better. It can cover pimples, lengthen lashes, and erase dark circles. It can make them look older or fancier. They think this way because they have been exposed to images that reinforce this throughout their entire lives.

Before beginning the conversation about makeup with your daughter, start by focusing on the things that make her beautiful: her gleaming smile or glowing skin or flowing hair. Encourage her to celebrate her natural features that other people are drawn to. We all have things we want to change about ourselves, sure, but we also have things that make us stand out. Help her to see these things, and model that by finding them in yourself. It takes a lot of pressure off the makeup conversation.

If your daughter is asking about makeup, address it, even if you think she's too young to wear it. Talk about how old you think she should be when she starts using it and explain why. Help her to understand that it doesn't always make someone look better or older. Some moms don't mind experimentation with makeup, particularly at home. If that's you, just remember to set limits. And keep your eye on what she's using, because you don't want her to use products that might cause skin reactions. You'll also want to teach her that sharing certain products—lip gloss or mascara, for example—can lead to sharing germs.

Concealer is probably the most common type of makeup that younger girls want to use, and with good reason: If a girl's skin is broken out, she may feel much better about herself if she can cover up her blemishes. If you are OK with concealer, help your daughter choose products that are good for her skin and that match her skin tone. And be sure to remind her to wash her face well after wearing any kind of product, because her skin will look healthier if she keeps it clean.

How to Say It?
"Some moms are OK with makeup at your age, but I'm not. I'm happy to explain why. And maybe there are some other things you can try if you want to change up your look, like a new hairstyle."

How to Say It?
"Before we talk about what you want to change with makeup, let's talk about what you like best about yourself. I love your sparkly eyes and wide smile. Now your turn."

How to Say It?
"I think it's fine to wear a little bright nail polish—but not lipstick yet. Let's take this one step at a time."

How to Say It?
"You seem really interested in wearing makeup lately. When I started, it was because I wanted to cover up pimples. Do you feel the same way? Or are you curious about other things like lip gloss and mascara because some of your friends wear those? I am happy to talk it through with you."

Clothing

Making choices that define her unique look is an important way for your daughter to express her growing independence. For many girls, it's also exciting to try clothes and products that feel more grown up. You want your daughter to feel beautiful. You want to encourage her creativity and imagination. At the same time, it's a mother's job to provide guidance. Unless a choice is clearly inappropriate or unhealthy, it's best to let her explore it, even if it's not to your taste. Then when you do need to say no, she will more likely understand that you are not trying to squash her individuality.

How to Say It?

"You have a great sense of style. Tell me about how you come up with such creative ways to combine your clothes and what styles you like these days. I'd love to hear about it."

At some point, your daughter's clothing choices will veer from your choices for her. While this is age appropriate and expected, it's often not easy for mothers, who have enjoyed choosing clothes they felt best suited their daughters. But what's most difficult are the disagreements that arise when she wants to buy or wear something that you find inappropriate, especially clothes that show too much in the way of skin or curves. This includes very short skirts and shorts, tightly fitted items, thin fabrics, and low-cut or strapless tops; it can also include padded bras and string bikinis.

Many parents feel that the clothing available for girls is too sexual and that the media make the problem worse. But if you tell your daughter that certain clothes are "inappropriate," she may conclude that you're too conservative, overprotective, or out of touch. Explaining your concern requires both specificity and delicacy. Try saying something like, "I want you to feel attractive and to express yourself. Unfortunately, clothing that's tight or shows a lot of skin can create impressions that you don't mean, and you're likely to get attention that you don't want. It's not your fault. But that's the way it is, and I want you to be safe. Let's find other clothes that you'll feel good in."

How to Say It?

"I know that those pants are popular right now, but sometimes pants that are tight can actually affect your body. When clothes are too constricting, you can get sweaty, rashy, or itchy."

Here are some additional tips for minimizing conflict:

Compliment her clothing and style choices.

Give sincere encouragement whenever you can: "That color looks so nice on you." "What a nice combination, that top and sweater." She'll know you share common ground, and your compliments will feel good. Ideally, she'll feel empowered to make more good choices like the ones you've noticed.

Give her latitude. Set a rule for yourself not to intervene when you don't like an outfit only for aesthetic reasons. If she's spending her own money, let her buy things that you know may not hold up well. If you're not sure something she's wearing will be exactly right for a place or event, think twice before saying something. She'll learn from her own experiences, and you won't feel or be perceived as overly critical.

Talk about "uniforms." Our culture expects certain kinds of clothing for certain times and places. During calm moments, discuss these outside expectations—what's considered appropriate for a nice restaurant, school and work, a job interview, a choir performance, and so forth. When the expectation is external, it's not about a mom's opinions or rules, so it's much easier to accept.

Avoid last-minute confrontations. Having a conversation about an outfit when your daughter is already dressed and heading out the door is stressful for everyone. Talk about what clothing is considered appropriate and allowed by her school. Have those chats about cultural expectations. Preview an outfit for a special occasion—and make it fun. Talk about the items in her wardrobe while you're doing laundry. Advance groundwork can prevent many arguments.

Choose your words carefully. Be specific when you reject an item or an outfit, and add a measure of affection. "Honey, that skirt is too short for school" is better than "You cannot wear that to school." Although she's not likely to be happy with the nicer version, she won't feel ashamed or humiliated and she'll know what the standard is for next time.

Find compromise where you can. Some items that are inappropriate in some circumstances might be more acceptable in others. And some outfits might be fine with a slight modification or addition. Work with her when possible, while still being firm about your basic rules of health and safety.

How to Say It?
"That's a cute tank top, but it's too casual for your volunteer job. How about putting a sweater over it? That will help with the cold air-conditioning, too."

How to Say It?
"Before you race out the door, I just noticed you're wearing a sundress that's backless. I know you said that everybody is wearing them now that it's warm outside, but it won't work for school—it's not within the guidelines. You'll need to find a jacket or sweater to go over the dress or make a quick outfit change."

Control & the Body

So much about a person is determined by inherited genes: not only hair, skin, and eye color but also height and build and even elements of personality and temperament. Where genes are in charge, we don't have control. Your daughter's genes are starting to reveal how tall and curvy she will be, how much hair she'll have, and more. Accepting the parts of herself that she can't change is a primary ingredient for her happiness and confidence throughout life. You can encourage this with your acceptance of both her genetic blueprint and your own.

On the other hand, there are many things about the body that we can and do control. People make lifestyle decisions throughout the day, including what and how much to eat and whether and how much to exercise. You may choose to listen to your body: Are you getting enough exercise? Or are you pushing too hard when you work out? Are you eating healthy foods? Are you eating enough? Or are you eating even though you're full? These choices add up to changing the way your body looks and feels. These choices also affect your health. Making the wrong choices can cause weight problems, which then lead to other health problems. The same is true for your daughter.

The terms *overweight* and *obesity* mean that a person weighs more than she should given how tall she is. Many people—both kids and adults—struggle with being

How to Say It?

"When I was at the pool today, I was thinking about how much I like the feeling of my legs powering me through the water. That got me thinking about how important it is to accept the bodies we're born with—to embrace what we like and make peace with what we wish was different. Have you ever noticed what great strength you have in your arms when you swing your tennis racket, and how good your eye-hand coordination is when you hit the tennis ball?"

Family Choices

Healthy choices are hard to manage alone. The best chance for success is to implement healthy changes for everyone in the house. The motivation might come from your daughter: When kids go through puberty, they sometimes have a new interest in what's going into their bodies. Honor this interest, and turn it into changes for the whole family. Talk to her about setting goals for the family, and then gradually change what's in your refrigerator or pantry to make healthy eating easier. At the same time, talk about physical activities you can do together or as a family, or encourage each other to do. The enthusiasm you share can make all the difference.

overweight. When kids work on this issue with their parents, as a family, it's easier for everyone to get healthier. If you want to talk about weight with your daughter, talk about it in terms of health, and figure out how you can work as a team to make lifestyle choices that will help everyone become healthier.

Eating disorders such as *anorexia* and *bulimia* often stem from a girl's desire to control what she eats. In the case of anorexia, the control is so intense that she cannot allow herself to eat enough calories to maintain a healthy weight. Bulimia is a failure to control; a girl is unable to stop herself from eating large amounts of food, and she then throws up or exercises excessively to get rid of the calories. Control issues related to food are unfortunately common, affecting tweens, teens, and adults of both genders.

If you think your daughter is trying to control what she eats because she wants to look a different way, it's critical to start a dialogue about it. You may need to try several times before she is willing to open up, but gently persist. In addition, make an appointment with her doctor for a checkup, and voice your concerns when you make the appointment and during the visit. Carrying around this secret is a heavy burden, and kids who don't acknowledge it and get help can become very sick.

If your daughter has any sort of weight problem—and even if she doesn't—your influence can be powerful and positive. Start by showing her that you appreciate and accept the body you were born with. Avoid making disparaging comments about your body, and instead focus on what you like, including what your body can *do*. Second, treat your body with respect by making healthy choices: good food and exercise in the right amounts. You are your daughter's number one role model.

The World Beyond

The world has changed radically over the past couple of decades, thanks in large part to the creation of the Internet. This technology has affected daily routines in fundamental ways, including everything from information access to time management to interpersonal connections. With the world literally at our fingertips, anyone can have a direct line to the outside world. As a result, today's kids must be taught how to use this technology wisely and safely.

Yet in spite of these dramatic shifts, when it comes to how kids feel and how they interrelate, things aren't so different from when you were growing up. Puberty is still a time when kids push for independence, and peer pressure and risk taking increase. Friendships change and romantic feelings emerge. Schedules fill up with new interests and increased schoolwork. Family tensions erupt as kids distance themselves one moment but want to feel included the next.

Regardless of the tools and methods, tweens and teens are heading out from their homes and beginning to make bigger decisions on their own. By now, they generally know right from wrong. This knowledge is something that parents, teachers, doctors, and other adult figures have worked to teach them throughout their lives. But the notion of right and wrong can blur in the tween years as friends influence one another's decisions.

Your daughter's brain is developing at the same time as her body. The limbic system, which is the center of emotions and desires, matures before the prefrontal cortex. It's the prefrontal cortex that weighs pros and cons, considers consequences, and delays gratification—and it won't be fully developed until she is in her 20s. This means that tweens are really good at making emotional choices, particularly choosing things that feel good in the moment or that impress their friends. But they are not as good at thinking through the results of those choices. The pressure to fit in and look cool can switch on the emotional center of the brain and cause your daughter to think about joining in, even overriding what she knows is smart, safe, or right.

Your daughter is moving into the world. Your job as her parent is to support that transition, letting her experience independence within age-appropriate bounds of safety. Many conversations with her will revolve around rules and limits that protect her safety while enabling her to grow and even make mistakes—giving her the practice she needs to make good choices. At the same time, you'll listen more, empathize with her, and offer loving encouragement at every opportunity. These are the ingredients for her successful passage into adulthood.

Family Scenes

Layered on top of all of the changes of puberty—physical, emotional, and social—are family dynamics. Tweens typically shift their focus away from parents and siblings to friends, and at home they begin to seek more privacy. This transition can be a little bumpy, as girls draw their family into their innermost circle one moment, then push them away the next.

As a parent, you may wonder how to navigate your daughter's shifts. How can you keep her integrated with the rest of the family while allowing her healthy pursuit of independence? And what's the best way to respond when she's out of sorts with family members?

How to Say It?

"I want you to have fun with your friends. I remember wanting more time with my friends when I was your age, too, and I don't think I was trying to juggle as much homework and other things as girls do now. Let's figure out where you can find more time to hang out with your friends, and still keep our most important family activities going."

How to Say It?

"You've been saying you need more privacy. Is something making it hard to get that? Do you have ideas about how to get more space and time for yourself? I'd like to help."

How to Say It?

"I know you're excited about getting a cell phone. It's a privilege that shows you're growing up, and we're excited for you. Before we buy it, though, we need to talk about how you'll use it. We're getting the phone so you can be in touch with us—to let us know where you are and to keep yourself safe. Let's go through our family rules for cell phones."

Despite appearances, your daughter wants to stay close to the family, even as she is focusing more on the world beyond home. Making sure the family has dinner together as often as possible and planning occasional gatherings that are just for fun go a long way toward keeping family members connected. Although she may complain, on a deeper level she'll be happy that she matters and

belongs. She will also be happier about family time if you let her know that you support her desire for independence and time with friends as well as her need for privacy.

In the meantime, when your daughter is embarrassed by you, irritable with siblings, argumentative, or remote, keep in mind that tweens are often as confused as you are about their changing moods and intense feelings. Rude or hurtful behavior should not be excused, but knowing this may help you respond more calmly and effectively.

Your daughter may ask that rules be modified if an older sibling had fewer restrictions at her age or if your daughter has the same restrictions as a younger sibling. She may not realize that restrictions are based not only on age but also on the child herself. Some kids need more oversight than others. When you talk with your daughter, help her understand that rule changes are the result of demonstrated responsibility and trustworthiness, not just age, and that she can look forward to fewer restrictions as she matures.

How to Say It?

"I've thought about your request for more screen time during the week, and I've decided this isn't the right time. I'm happy to talk about it again when summer comes and you don't have homework. I'm sure you're disappointed, and we can certainly talk about those feelings. The bottom line, though, is that I need to do what I think is best for you, because that's my job as your mom."

How to Say It?

"I know it's common for kids to have more intense feelings and sometimes feel moody at this age. I do remember feeling that way myself. But snapping at your family doesn't help you feel better. It actually can make you feel worse, because it adds to your stress. Let's talk about what's going on that's causing you to feel bad and find better ways to deal with it."

Family Talk

During puberty, kids often start thinking about big family issues like adoption or divorce. It is common for them to question what happened or where they came from. If the family configuration isn't traditional, they'll want to talk about that, too. These conversations are deeply meaningful and may evolve over months or years, strengthening a girl's sense of self and belonging. They are sensitive, so proceed carefully and be honest but not negative—keeping in mind that your daughter's feelings may be very different from your own.

Social Shifts

Your daughter's friends are more important than ever, now that she's older. She spends more time with them, shares experiences with them, and learns from them.

And friends can change fast. The combination of things like school workload, clubs and activities, cliques, and crushes often pushes girls in different directions. Your daughter might grow apart from a friend who has been close for years while finding new friends who share common interests. These shifts feel exciting, yet sad and confusing, too.

As her focus moves to her friends, their influence increases. She'll want to please them. She'll want to do the things people her age are doing—or at least the things they say they're doing. And if her friends are pressuring her, she may find it hard to resist going along, even if she knows it's a bad idea.

Because of this influence and the power of peer pressure, it's important to be able to identify a good friend. As an adult, you're usually able to gauge a person's intentions and authenticity—you've had years of practice. Your daughter hasn't. Parents often struggle with what to do when their daughter develops a friendship with someone who may be a bad influence. It's important to raise your concerns in the most nonjudgmental way possible, and then present her with boundaries you feel need to be in place around that friendship.

How to Say It?

"It's hard when friends talk about a movie they've seen. But I don't think it's appropriate to see PG-13 movies in the theater, since you're 10. If there's a movie you'd like to rent, I'm willing to preview it and see if you can watch, with me fast-forwarding if any parts are too advanced."

How to Say It?

"It's a tough situation when friends want you to exclude someone. I know how important your friends are to you, and nobody wants to worry about losing friends. But I also know how much you value being a nice person—and I'm proud of you for that. Is this a time when something simple like the golden rule could guide you?"

Mantras for Moms

1. If other kids claim they're doing something, it's not necessarily true.

2. If I don't want my daughter doing something, chances are good that most other parents don't either.

3. If my daughter doesn't get to do something, she may be upset at first, but ultimately she'll be OK and maybe even better off.

Tweens and teens share a great deal with each other, but of course other kids aren't always the best source of advice or information—even when they mean well. While allowing your daughter the space to grow with her friends, you also want to be viewed as a source of reliable information and guidance. Listening more and holding back with some of your opinions and suggestions are part of your own transition.

But what if you're concerned about what you're hearing from your daughter? Start by listening with empathy and without judgment. Then share your concerns and offer the wisdom and guidance your daughter sometimes needs at this age. While we like to think she'll be talking and thinking things through for herself, arriving at wiser conclusions on her own, that is an ideal to strive for. She may need a little help from you to get there.

How to Say It?
"I'd like to talk about your friend Bee. I can see how funny and energetic she can be, and why you really like her. But I'm concerned about some of the things I've heard her say and the way she dresses like an older girl. I'm not comfortable with you going to her house, but if you'd like to invite her here once in a while, that's OK. Have you noticed these things about Bee? How do you feel about them?"

Bullying
Bullying no longer happens just on the playground or the walk home. Today it exists online, too, and around the clock. Although a bully might be one person or a small group, the ceaseless torment can make a girl feel more alone and hopeless than ever.

Your daughter needs to know what to do if she or someone she knows is being bullied. Asking for help is a sign of strength, but bullies count on kids being afraid that telling will make things worse. Encourage your daughter to get help from a trusted adult where the bullying is happening, and ease her fears about the bullying getting worse if addressed. If the bullying is taking place at school, get involved in the school's plan to stop it. Ask specifically, "How will you intervene so that my daughter is kept out of it and the bullying doesn't get worse?" Reassure your daughter that teachers and other adults know how to deal effectively with bullying.

Your daughter also needs to know what constitutes bullying so that she's not doing it herself. Help her learn to imagine the consequences of an action and to put herself in another's place. Sometimes a girl does something she thinks is silly or harmless, when in reality she causes someone great distress.

Virtual Worlds

These days, the word *friend* has many different meanings. A friend used to be a person you knew rather well and in the flesh. But now it can refer to someone you connect with through social media—maybe you only sort of know them, or maybe you've just seen their picture and read their profile. Today, "friends" can actually be total strangers.

For this reason and more, most social media sites don't allow members under the age of 13. Age limits help protect the safety and the personal information of minors. Keeping young kids off these sites can help them avoid early exposure to online bullying, sexting, and other inappropriate content. More than that, tweens are not yet able to fully understand the power of these sites or the consequences of their behavior on them. It's hard to grasp that words and pictures can be seen by millions of people—people you might not want knowing your thoughts and personal information, people who might not use that information in a good way. It's also hard to realize that the instant something is posted, it's out of your control forever. You can never take it back—not ever. "Think before you post" is a vital lesson to learn before being allowed to sign up and sign on.

How to Say It?

"I know you'd like an account even though you're not 13 yet. I understand it seems like everyone else is on the site but you. I'm sure there are girls under 13 who have accounts—including girls whose parents let them join without telling their true age. But we are not going to let you sign up until you're 13. It's important that you know we're going to follow the rules and expect you to do the same. The rules keep kids safe, and we take that very seriously."

Think Before Posting!

Review these questions with your daughter—more than once—and suggest that she post them on the computer screen.

1. Would I want my mom (my teacher, the people I work for, the college I want to go to) to see this picture or this thing I am about to say?

2. Could this cause any kind of problem for me, my family, or someone else—either now or in the future?

3. Could someone figure out who I am or where I live if I post this?

4. Would it be better to send this in a private message or e-mail instead of making it public?

Social Media Contract

- ☑ I will not sign up for any site without my parents' OK.
- ☑ My parents and I will preview a site together before deciding to sign me up.
- ☑ My parents and I will register for my account and set privacy settings together, and I will not change any settings myself.
- ☑ My parents will have the usernames and passwords to any accounts I have.
- ☑ My parents will "friend" and "follow" me on all my sites and will be able to see everything I post.
- ☑ I will never post my last name, my home address, the name of my school, or other information that identifies me or my family—either in words or in pictures.

_____   _____
Daughter   Mom

There are many good reasons for enforcing age rules. First, it helps you keep your daughter safe. Also, it helps keep everyone in your family safe, it helps other parents enforce the rule with their children, and it teaches children to respect rules. Enforcing this one in her tween years sets the important precedent that you will follow rules and laws in future situations that arise with your daughter (such as those around driving and alcohol), and it tells her that you expect her to do the same.

When she does reach the allowed age—and you decide that a site is appropriate and safe for her—that decision is only the first step. Before your daughter signs up for any social media sites, consider writing a contract. List the sites she is allowed to join, be specific about the rules (see the suggestions above), and outline the consequences if she doesn't follow through. Ultimately, when kids have specific rules and when they know their parents are seeing their activity, they are far more likely to make smart decisions in the virtual world.

How to Say It?
"You're old enough now to have an account—congratulations! Before you sign up, we need to talk about ways to stay safe with social media, not just on this site but also any others we give you permission for. Some rules go with this privilege, and I've put them in a contract. Let's look at the contract together and go through each point. Then we'll both sign it."

Romance

The social changes facing tweens extend beyond friendships, both real and virtual. For many girls—maybe your daughter, maybe her friends—they involve romantic stirrings as well.

The feeling of a pounding heart or a hot face can take a tween by surprise. A normally articulate girl can find herself suddenly tongue-tied—then embarrassed or baffled. Some girls don't develop these feelings until they are older, while others have crushes even as young children. But one thing is certain: The emotions intensify during puberty.

How to Say It?

"When girls start liking someone, it's really normal to question your feelings or wonder what's OK. The best advice I can give you is to trust how you feel. If he wants to hold your hand but you're not ready, or if you're not sure you have those feelings for him, or if you don't want to be affectionate in front of your friends, it's best to wait. Tell him what you're feeling. Honest conversation is important in any friendship, and liking someone is really just a special form of friendship. Talking will help you get to know him better and will help you get clearer about how you feel."

Parents sometimes shy away from conversations about crushes, because they're worried they might open the door to inappropriate thoughts, words, and behaviors. The hope is that if they avoid these conversations, those feelings will fizzle out or not appear at all. But neither of these is true. Talking about feelings doesn't encourage sexual behavior, nor does it accelerate a girl's maturation. Instead, it helps your daughter sort out her confusing feelings and learn to behave in ways that feel right for her and are appropriate for her age.

How to Say It?

"When a friend starts liking someone, it's natural to feel a bit left out. Just try saying what you're feeling in a positive way, like, 'Isabel, I love being friends and I miss hanging out with you. It's great that you like someone, but maybe you don't realize how little time you've had with your friends lately. Do you think we can go to the movies this weekend like we used to?'"

One day, romantic relationships will be a big part of her life, and opening the dialogue now will serve her well for years to come. You want her to feel that she can ask questions and get accurate information. You want her to feel comfortable sharing her excitements and disappointments. You want her to talk through the kinds of people she's drawn to and how she feels with them. The earlier these conversations start, the more natural they will feel. If she shares innocent crushes in elementary school, she's more likely to talk about a more serious relationship in high school or college. In fact, as your daughter gets older, her need for basic information about healthy living and body changes will diminish, but conversations about love and romance have no end.

How to Say It?

"Girls are often trying to figure out who they like, but it's also important to know how to choose that special person. It helps to remember what you learned about picking good friends when you were younger, because it's not any different. Look for someone who's kind to you, and caring and respectful to everyone. Honesty is big, too. Most of all, pick someone you can be yourself with, and who makes you feel great when you're together."

How to Say It?

"Maybe the next time Emma talks about Ethan you can just take a casual approach and say, 'He's really nice, and I can see why you like him.' It's probably easiest not to mention that you like him, too, but inside you can feel anything you like. Being friends with lots of different boys and girls is good right now. At this age, feelings change all the time, and everyone will have lots of crushes and relationships. Remembering that will probably help your friendships go more smoothly."

Heart to Heart

1. Be empathetic. Empathy shows your daughter that you understand and that you think her feelings are important. Don't tease or dismiss her feelings as juvenile. If you show respect and caring now, she'll continue to share when she's older and her feelings run deeper.

2. Listen and give your daughter the chance to share openly. Silences can feel awkward and embarrassing to tweens, though, so if you sense that happening, offer a caring comment or a brief sharing of your own relevant experience at her age.

3. Avoid judging her feelings or seeming critical. If you're concerned that she likes someone who doesn't seem right for her or she's too focused on superficial traits, offer a supportive comment and share your concern as neutrally as possible. You might say, "It sounds like Jake is really cute, but it also sounds like you don't like how he treats less popular kids. Do you think everyone's getting carried away with how popular and cute he is but losing sight of what he's really like as a person?"

43

Time Management

It's not uncommon for tweens to feel overextended. A girl involved with a couple of activities can suddenly find her afternoons and evenings crammed with practices and rehearsals piled on top of her increasing home-work load. There's little time for friends, family, chores, or just unwinding. Sleep may suffer, too.

All kids need help learning to manage their time and commitments. Your life experience will provide valuable insights about such basics as getting orga-nized, doing first things first, and saying no—even to things a person likes. Your daughter's activities and proj-ects might be worthwhile, but maybe they're more than she can handle. It will be a relief for her if you help her figure out how she can hold it all together or lighten her load.

There might be additional wrinkles. What if your daughter really wants to do an activity, but logistics, cost, or safety is a concern? Or what if her skills or interests are different from yours and you can't relate to her passion—or she's not interested in something you've picked for her? Before you redirect her away from her passion, talk it through. Discuss prac-tical or safety concerns, and get information. If your concerns can be resolved, it's in her best interest to pursue something that excites her. Girls who have a significant interest or activity tend to have the easiest time getting through puberty and the teen years. This can be a sport, a music or dance activity, an after-school club—just about anything. What matters is that she likes it enough to stick with it and she feels good about contributing to something meaningful or mastering the skills involved.

On the other hand, what if your daughter wants to quit an activity she asked for? Should she stop or stick it

How to Say It?
"I'M glad you told me how you feel, and I'M happy to help. Sometimes making a schedule and organizing your calendar makes things feel more in control. We could also research time-management strategies online."

How to Say It?
"I know you're frustrated with softball and that you wish you could quit. I get that there are a lot of practices and you're not happy with your coach. But it's important that you follow through on the commitment you've made to your teammates and finish out the season. Once it's ended, you don't have to continue. And if there's anything we can do to help make it more fun, please let me know."

out? It depends. Here are a few questions to consider and discuss together:

* Does she have too much on her plate? Does something need to be discontinued because she is indeed overextended?

* Why has she lost interest? Is it the activity itself—or another factor, such as an instructor she doesn't care for?

* Does she have a pattern of quitting? Staying with something because you said you would, for a reasonable amount of time such as a season or semester—even when it's not fun at the moment—is an important life skill to acquire.

* Has she lost faith in herself? Sometimes kids (and adults) want to give up when something gets hard, but if they work through it, they're glad they did.

* Did you pay a lot for this activity? Cost is a consideration, but it must be viewed in the context of her feelings.

* Is she part of a team or club, with others depending on her participation?

* Does she have at least one other activity—or an alternative in mind to take the place of the one she wants to stop?

How to Say It?

"I'M glad you told me you aren't enjoying piano lessons. I wonder if it's been bothering you for a while. It's really OK to tell me if an activity doesn't seem right for you. Music is a fine pursuit, but there are lots of other great things. As soon as you finish this set of lessons that we've already paid for, we can look into other activities you might like better."

Top Time-Management Tips

1. Look online together for time-management ideas that appeal to your daughter, and help her put her favorites in place.

2. Review her schedule every week at a regular time, and help her plan ahead.

3. Encourage her to get ready the night before.

4. Help her make a place for things—her backpack, her equipment, her supplies—to help her stay organized.

Comm-YOU-nication

Puberty isn't something your daughter needs to experience alone. While the goal is independence, it's a gradual process that's meant to take years. Your job is to help her through these years by keeping her healthy and safe, by loving her and showing her how to love herself, and by giving her the information and decision-making skills she'll need as an adult.

Share your stories when your daughter is open to hearing them, in ways that are relevant to her. Listen when she wants to talk. Impart your wisdom, having faith that she heard you—even if it doesn't seem that way. Your relationship is unique, and there's no "right" way to communicate. Just take the time you need to find ways that work well for the two of you.

Every adult has been through puberty. We all have unique memories and advice. Encourage your daughter to collect stories from other trusted adults, too, learning from their collective experiences. The most valuable advice comes from people who have her best interests at heart. As your daughter's mother, you are at the top of that list.

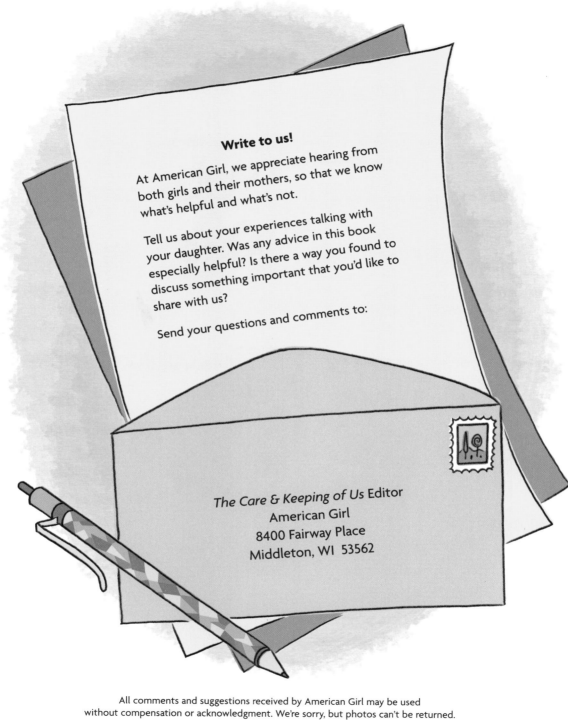

Write to us!

At American Girl, we appreciate hearing from both girls and their mothers, so that we know what's helpful and what's not.

Tell us about your experiences talking with your daughter. Was any advice in this book especially helpful? Is there a way you found to discuss something important that you'd like to share with us?

Send your questions and comments to:

The Care & Keeping of Us Editor
American Girl
8400 Fairway Place
Middleton, WI 53562

All comments and suggestions received by American Girl may be used without compensation or acknowledgment. We're sorry, but photos can't be returned.

Here are some other American Girl books you might like:

Each sold separately. Find more books online at americangirl.com.